invisible bride

WINNER OF THE WALT WHITMAN AWARD FOR 2003

Sponsored by The Academy of American Poets, the Walt Whitman Award is given annually to the winner of an open competition among American poets who have not yet published a book of poems.

Judge for 2003: C. D. Wright

invisible bride

[p o e m s]

tony tost

louisiana state university press   baton rouge   2004

Designer: Amanda McDonald Scallan
Typeface: Sabon
Printer and binder: Thomson-Shore, Inc.

Library of Congress Cataloging-in-Publication Data:
Tost, Tony.
  Invisible bride : poems / Tony Tost.
       p. cm.
  ISBN 0-8071-2964-X (cloth : alk. paper) — ISBN 0-8071-2965-8 (pbk. : alk. paper)
  I. Title.
  PS3620.O88I58 2004
  811'.6—dc22
                                        2003019397

Some of the poems in this volume first appeared, sometimes in slightly different form, in the following
publications: *American Poet; Black Warrior Review; Born; can we have our ball back?; Fence; Field;
Forklift, Ohio; Good Foot; La Petite Zine; Localist; No: a journal of the arts; Pleiades; Quarter After
Eight; Spinning Jenny; storySouth; Typo.*

The author would like to thank: Ron and Teresa Tost, his family, Tara Bray, Sami Buffington, Michael
Heffernan, Zach Schomburg, Paul White, C.D. Wright, all Arkansas writers and rockers, the Vermont
Studio Center, the Academy of American Poets, the University of Arkansas Creative Writing program,
and Carolyn Walton for her support of the program. And (above all) Leigh Plunkett.

For Don & Ethel
For Anne & Frank

My dear Fanny I am ashamed of writing you such stuff, nor would I if it were not for being tired after my day's walking, and ready to tumble into bed so fatigued that when I am asleep you might sew my nose and trundle me round the town like a Hoop without waking me—Then I get so hungry.

—JOHN KEATS

1

The man's Vision begins with the child's Sob.

Who shall say what one's Vision has to offer another? Yet, in many cases, Vision's path is presented with such singular exactness of fidelity that we are perfectly safe in submitting the minds of even the youngest children to its influence: the gatehouse *will* hold firm and keep out the invaders, and the fires *shall* illuminate the archers manning the battlements.

Fire is indeed a sweet and proper vision for children; it is most instructive and fascinating, and forms a realistic preparation for the afterlife, with a more serene and thoughtful appreciation of its meaning. We might fan our flames by a thousand and one simple observations; for instance, that the same sun which ripens my beans illumines an inner ward which is a nightmare of smoke and flames and the screams of horses and men.

I have joined the line of men passing buckets of water from the well to the fire, which was not my original vision: O visible stars at the apex of invisible triangles!

Distant and different beings in the various mansions of Vision are often contemplating the same face at the same hour, and yet our visions are as varied as our names. Sometimes we can pretend we don't see the visions, but this just makes the headaches worse.

Can a greater miracle take place than to feel the pain in another's head, if only for an instant?

This is what the sobbing child is trying to say—what it is always trying to say—but this time, we tell ourselves, we can do something. We fling open the doors to our rooms and race down the corridors. Our eyes water from the smoke. Although our skin is hot, a sudden chill works through, and our only desire is to groan aloud. This is the exact moment when we should not. Enemies are waiting outside; they grin and reach into their incredibly long robes. They hate the robes but are able to have many hidden pockets sewn into them. From these pockets they pull swords.

First of all, a war closes its eyes and moves stiffly towards the present. If I insist upon this image, it is because I see in it a kind of surrender.

A war, to be considered realistic, must draw blood. (It is said of certain wars that they are speechless.) We know that war cannot be reduced to simple killing; we are all committed to conflict and define ourselves by it. Hence, the most interesting sights, e.g., a woman's face, are presented as struggles.

Perhaps this is disturbing. The present power of a past war is measured by the detours it has imposed upon traditional ideals—man is essentially good, and so on.

There are two means of demystifying a great war: by making it the predetermined product of a moment, or by reducing it to a single image (Hell) or word/phrase ("Vietnam" "great war").

War reveals a more sensual side of history. It has at least two faces: one which, if not attractive, is at least inquisitive. Also, the face of an imbecile. Nature itself—sea, mountain—is nothing but the human body in expansion and, one's face might say, in conflict. Everything suggests there is no escape: in a state of conflict, events fit into one another like a woman fits into a dress.

There is no temptation to call this another form of surrender.

For years, irate mothers' groups have demanded playground reform as child-guidance experts, educators, architects and artists formulated the exact number of dangerous illusions in the world. For openers, the lakes appear to be sheathed in glass while it is in fact the dreary expanses of asphalt that are stuffed with it.

Two swing-sets are nearly touching.

A playground lets our children dash about—willing, laughing, suspending, breaking each other's bones—as the thinkers make fools of us. The playground spins our thoughts around and extends a hospitable welcome to those who want to avail themselves of a chance to walk in the shade of some excellent exterior landscaping. This month, I will explore playground reform as an intuitive response aiming to produce and promote ideal gender identities in children.

A child's body itself is a playground in which gender identities can be monitored and produced, compelling reformers (yours truly) to locate them in public, visible settings. Like a cloud, I am meant to serve a large population. A playground should be a sort of truce between the tunnels and twilights of childhood. A playground should be rippling at its outermost branches. According to the Consumer Product Safety Commission, about 120,000 playground injuries are treated in U.S. hospitals each year.

A playground should remain in a child's heart, even as that child, years later, awakes, in his or her own clothes, on a beach, bruised (in a "pool of bruises" in fact), blue-veined and delivered from his or her indolence into an outdoor, multi-use play area of a completely different sort, one that unambiguously acknowledges a community's commitment to its children and the future they will inherit.

A playground, above all else, should be the first blossom *and* the wintry ground, the fuzzy, distant shore *and* the whale's belly, the physical soup *and* the philosophical skin that agrees to mouth adult expectations concerning aesthetics and safety, even as it swallows them.

My father traveled a lot, railroading as a Pullman porter and working at sea. My father traveled in circles. My father traveled the Pacific Ocean establishing radio stations that would be of great use during the war. He traveled north for months at a time. Increasingly, my father traveled in solitude.

When I was a child my bed was large and I, like a compass, turned in the night to face whatever direction I believed my father was headed. When I was fifteen I traveled with him for a week, and my mother stayed home and slept in my clothes.

When my father came home from another country he called me the word for "doll" in that country's language. At night, according to my mother, he could travel into the heart of disaster. My father traveled thousands of kilometers by train through the endless landscapes of Russia, Mongolia and China. He documented this voyage with dozens of tiny cuts across the back of a small doll.

In one letter, he wrote "every child is a Negro hung in chains on a tree."

It has been said that to be a father is to be traveling at all times, through areas of holiness, and by so doing, acquiring holiness: when my father talked of God he pointed not at the sky but at his feet.

My father traveled to Kansas to find the Negro's gravesite but was unable to locate it. He traveled long distances by horse, riding by night and sometimes herding animals. "My argument," my father wrote, "is not with the dark, but with those who stumble in it."

One year he sent home small machines from all over the country, and my mother and I would drag each to the river. There was snow all over the ground. More than once I burst into tears at his accounts of traveling the country in railway cars and playing the devil at hoedowns in order to stay alive.

When my father finally returned, I slept in my boots.

My twin died at birth. The clouds weighed ten ounces. The clouds were cold, hard facts. Father carried me in one arm and a doll in the other. The doll, as a ritual, was fed daily. The clouds were secrets never to be discussed. The clouds were bundled in red light. The doll always seemed hungry, so Father made a second doll with two mouths. The clouds were numb, reckless. I dyed my hair black and then I started my first fire. The smoke had a green tinge and looked tired. The clouds were light and dark portraits and hawks darted into and back into the clouds. I started sleeping in the kitchen. The clouds were always the same three colors. I started my second fire in late summer. The clouds were a color I called strawberry-flame. The doll fell into a pot of boiling water. I made a new fire, for Father to sing to.

A Halo Best Described as Oceanic

1.

What joy is it now to set a table, to walk beneath cherry blossoms, to spend an hour at the arcade? November gives a perverse taste. December has never given me the desire to say simple things. January and February are two spurs practicing the arts of coming, of going, often leading to a change of weather. It's late February and change has manifested a critical attitude in the locals towards cloud formations. There's so many local troubles: water being used so carefully, as if it had some real function, some sort of tradition.

2.

If March was intended to be a black comedy, it never finds its rhythm. Instead of building tension around the horrific events it can never escape, April is content with a rose-colored tint. May is so perfectly mousy. Decisions are often impossible. I can't decide how serious I want to be. How I should look into the water. What kinds of questions to ask: "How much does it cost to get a tattoo? How should I act once I get a tattoo?"

3.

Something bad happens every year in June and I am disappointed that it happens during June and not to June directly. Last summer I saw a woman drink from a glass that a dog had just used. A wish for water is sometimes enough. It is never enough. I almost drowned as a child but cannot remember the event, no matter how often my family tries to remind me.

4.

Upon witnessing a horse being whipped, Nietzsche threw his arms around the horse's neck and collapsed, never to return. I too live in the clouds, only to find myself thirsty. "And yet," one may ask, "have I contemplated the clouds for long enough? Who wants to stand in front of his house and point at the clouds?" I do! And me boss!

5.

Of all the months, July may be the one: freshness, and youth, and yet: it does not tell me how to explain the intricacies of aging. Aging appears to be one of many crowns. There may be more than one legitimate heir to a crown. It's absurd to deny a crown, but when I was ten months old I knew I wanted to walk. I've been walking ever since.

6.

"This August," one may declare, "I shall be transported to the river above or the river below." August, of course, is a simple formal dichotomy between rainy and non-rainy days. Wet and dry thoughts. The more time a man spends in the water, the heavier he gets. It rains and his breathing gets heavy. For example, every September he falls out of love but finds himself damp with thoughts of love. Like nature, he must learn to sing to himself.

Aging is the great escape: the angry climb out of innocence and its valleys full of long shadows and fleshy birds on the way to adulthood, which is an airport.

"God created airports because he needed to tell stories," Agnes tells me as we set up our tent in the woods a few minutes from town. She says an airport is a booth for pilgrims, a place to surrender the securities and simplicities of home (I still tell myself this when I am wandering beneath the artificial lights) even if a man is on a precise schedule and is quite clearly on his way home.

Agnes works at the airport as a waitress.

This is why we are out here in the woods, preparing our tent, leaving one side open to receive a surprise visitor, or the winds of prophecy, or the scent of baked trout.

"Every airport has its own rules," Agnes tells me, "signs guiding the lost towards more useful and fruitful tangents."

I've settled on Agnes as the otherworldly force that silently and insistently explains my reason for being. She theorizes about the sanctity of airports, which, she says, should be another word for "the right hand of God" since they usher His children into the clouds, or into a faraway land-of-lands, or, simply, away.

"If a person is sincerely humble," she says, "the airport will keep its lanes simple and free so the traveler may be escorted without a problem. But if the traveler is arrogant, the airport has been known to clutter and confuse itself so the traveler must either wait uncomfortably or suck in his gut, his worldly arrogance, so he may pass through the gates."

Often Agnes worries me. But sometimes Agnes is the sign pointing up the road, telling me to drive past Roger's Rec and Regina's House of Dolls and Finger Park and Lake Keith, to go ahead and cruise the airport parking lot, even if she's not working, if only to check out the planes that I will board drunkenly and with determination one day, so that I will be in the air, which will be (I am told) one more good place to enjoy a meal, to have someone tell me a story.

2

My first ambition was to make a film to be premiered on a small black and white television set, in the middle of a party, on a kitchen counter, and muted, which would be no problem at all, for the film would have been shot without sound anyway. The actors would not even pretend to be talking. For a time I thought the noise of the party could substitute for the lack of sound: dropped bottles, sing-a-longs, heavy breathing—a constant sense of novelty which, if one does not abandon it, leads to a sort of peace, which then turns into a monotony interrupted only by interludes of quiet, which are now, of course, charged. At this point, my film would be shown, but without any dialogue in the film the party-people would be forced to talk to one another, which is always a disaster. But I think they wouldn't mind the lack of sound if they understood the visual language: open curtains means the heroine has second thoughts, ducks on the pond and we know the hero is still alive, and so on. A lover gives the other a cross-eyed look, which means: "I can't believe you are afraid to die."

"For all the talk of shadows, we are mostly blood," the dead hostage tells me. He has forgiven the guerrillas who captured him and held him for two years before executing him in front of a video camera. His theory: when something is forgiven, it means that that thing is disposed of, that it no longer matters. The dead hostage tells me that he was held, with another man, in a shack without running water or electricity. He felt less isolated after the other man died, quietly, in his sleep, six months before he himself would die. He says: "Once alone in nature, no one spoke to me, nothing else had a will of its own, and my identity was limited only to what I could perceive. I did not have to imagine my identity, for it was visible, it had color and made noises all through the night." He means the ferns and the clouds that were visible from the shack, the rats that snuck into the shack, the spirituals he hummed, even the guerrillas off in the distance, even the heat—all of this was his identity. "It was showing itself to me," he says, "like an animal brushing against your face at night." He tells me that he was fed once a day, but the hunger that he felt was also a part of his identity—a physicality so distinct that it had a spiritual effect.

"Like what happens to an incredibly tall man," he says, "or a woman born with flippers." He embraced his hunger to such a degree that he could still feel it now that he was deceased. "To not carry it with me," he says, "would be like the ghost of Bette Davis tearing out its eyes."

Satisfaction was imposed upon every American. Sunday morning was a nail to the temple. They built a forest in the oval office and I lost my virginity in the shadows. The big fish was reeled in on Main Street. We threw it up. My dad fell off the wagon and all I got was this lousy t-shirt. Trail of the century. The true umbrella was lost. There was nothing behind the curtain except some great tits and a few thousand skulls. My mom held a snake before my window and I drew the picture. There was the comedian's ass, the letter-sea. Dad had a black rag for a lung. One evening before nightfall the cameramen stepped before their cameras. Each told one true story. Only the magazines remembered this (we could not remember a thing). It was a new universe every week. Astral suburbs. My parents and I took turns singing ourselves to sleep. We got better insulation for the house, a bigger fridge. We left our knives at the water's edge. Dad kept an extra knife at home. My neighbor got married in a torn skirt and the newspapers grew dark with wisdom. Two out of three Americans believed they were the eighth wonder of the world. The press did not fear God, only the necessity of one. I was afraid of the shirt my mother wanted me to wear. Yoko forgave us, we forgave her. It was our *White Album:* a long lazy sip as the new guard finds the switch.

Our waitress is aroused. She glides above our pale and incandescent heads. More than the scent of one's self there's the smell of dusk. Above our pale and incandescent heads: the evening is like a quiet skirmish (the smell of dusk spreading like butter on ham). The evening is, like, quiet. Squeamish. Moonlight is spilling into the punchbowl and spreading, like butter on ham. A strange new delicacy. "Impossible! Moonlight is spilling into the punchbowl!" I think, watching the evening transform into a strange new delicacy. Impossible not to think of one's self in these moments.

Once, I thought watching the world transform was some obscure brand of blessing, or to not think of one's self in these moments was a way of loving the world, that some obscure brand of blessing (or at least a vague answer) was in order, that forgetting was a way of loving the world. Now I just blush and ask questions, thinking at least a vague answer is in order.

Forgetting the night's quiet (that simple hush and glow), I, blushing, begin asking questions, thinking of things to think about between bites:

"The night's quiet." Something simple, hushed. Aglow.

"I enjoy the scent of night falling."

The things one thinks about between bites help one's companions eat in comfort:

"I enjoy the scent of night falling more than the scent of myself."

"One should help one's companions eat in comfort."

"Our waitress is a Rose."

"She glides."

Winter Outtakes (1)

1.

Illusory, ethereal productions, wistful melodies, and an oft-funereal pace: winter absorbs a man in such a way as to nearly dissolve the wolf inside him.

2.

I don't know (but I've been told) that what we see as color (I am currently noting how a moth, with its wing pattern, may mime a dead leaf) is in fact the amount of energy in the light meeting the eyes.

I don't know. I was told that animals, at night, certainly do weep—that it is from sorrow. For years cardinals have attacked the windows of my house. Every summer. Last spring. Winter also finds ways to punish its prisoners.

3.

Light reflects off the snow and into my eyes. I am the quality of this reflection. This attitude towards nature is quite recent for me (I have problems believing in heaven, but not wolves).

4.

My boys, given a small supply of water and food, are told where to build. Stuttering-heart cold. I sit in here and view musicals set in the 17th and 18th centuries, wondering how people occupied time other than killing, kissing, and writing letters.

We've all got questions: "Where's the fortune at the end?" Exactly. The point of Song—to get it wrong, to tear separately and separately; always *that* house, *those* heights, but *these* spirituals (which, I repeat, *are* incorrect).

So here are the incorrect signals, the pebbles that come out of a dog that talks, that decides to divine to the world what is important, what is not. The right rivers in the correct tunnels.

5.

A complete record is one request. A man can only remember the general impression of how a thing appears and cannot possibly recall all the details. If a terrain is especially severe, or exposed to a severity, why not map it from the air? (The camera is located in the belly of the craft.)

6.

Winter grows the more it talks. A woman's hair can go past her waist. It is unaware that it is wretched. Winter substantiates itself in the actuality of the chill it speaks. Winter grows. It seems pleased by the idea that its chill is our fate and must therefore be our practice. My boys will come inside sometimes and leave snow-puddles by the door, their ears beet-red, their noses too. Their sweaters are often dark, their conversations knowing.

7.

The story of children in the snow, of being chased by winter but seldom getting caught, is actually the story of me being chased by my own childhood; of how my childhood always escapes and becomes a part of the "collective memory" when I, after years of running and ducking, suddenly turn to chase *it*.

8.

Just yesterday my boys carried rocks back and forth in the frost, then came home and made some sleep.

As a child I spent my mornings learning. Currents, for example. They have no boundaries; there is no point at which moving water is in contact with water that is stationary. Instead, there are turbulent regions where frictions take place. I believe it. I'd do anything to feel weightless again.

9.

Winter remains, even after its pleasures surface, burst. Winter can turn us to knots, then turn its back and call out, waiting for us to put our masks back on so it can see who we really are.

10.

Thesis: the sea heats up slower than the land but retains its warmth longer.

Antithesis: people make their own clouds on a cold day, simply by exhaling.

Synthesis: we all have means of demanding attentiveness

but the world belongs to the seasons as well. Something in a winter scene absorbs us, and in our bemusement we discover unexpected but apt meaning there:

a snowman (we are, in fact, constructed by fantastic amounts of water and, rather like ping-pong balls violently supported by a fountain, we are liable to fall, swiftly, to the ground, in a cloudburst) or a sleeping dog.

11.

I suspect the borders would not be, for instance, between winter and spring, but between winter and snow: but this sort of talk is what caused the little girl in me to wander off in the first place.

I've spent the last few winters (treading softly, at all hours) patiently seeking that girl, and her favor. This winter I will hide and let *her* learn to hunt for me, let *her* brave the cold in her wond'red gown, let *her* whisper seriously.

The man who went into a coma after the flood is still out of it. We have similar needs. He moves through songs of sorrow and death ropes with a halo best described as 'oceanic.' This entire experience has been like watching the union of two virgins: him and the world (virgins are made for lying down together).

Since he dozed off, I have hoped to impress his mind that reality is a balanced bird with many equally important sections; that we should recognize and search for desirable traits and not be overly concerned with minor faults; that in the evaluation of the bird, a judge cannot help but feel dizzy.

I have used his senses as my weapon. I have made a mix-tape of disparate bird calls and allowed pigeons to nest in his bed.

For five weeks I have been teaching him to draw birds by taking his (cold, unresponsive) hand and executing some modest, semi-realistic sketches (each bird's neck tilted slightly back with no trace of neck-shaking or over-styling, all birds evenly colored throughout) of birds in their natural habitats.

I am very eager to judge his drawings when he finally awakes.

Points will be taken off for: a bird leaning too far forward or backward; head not held high; neck drawn too far back; dull or faded color, color lacking sheen; colors blending together to produce impure or smutty effect; bronze cast on body, neck or head; coarse, prominent, or contrasting ceres (except in white schietti, where a red cere is desired); pale or lusterless eye color; pinched in face; beetle brows; drooped eye lids; head too small for balance; scissored wings; loose feathers or long feathers; any tail or wing missing; excessive color; soft feathers; stained or soiled feathers; awry tail; tail too long; body too shallow, lacking depth; crooked keel; keel too long and not curved; body too small, lacking in substance; body too square or angular lacking overall roundness; broken bill or unmatched eyes; split keel; completely white primary or secondary wing feathers; completely white tail feathers.

My beard is a bridge between my past and my face. I have shaved with a supreme carelessness. My beard of sugar is in the rain. My beard of regrets.

There is a rumor of a beard that leans towards the West. California is flooded in beards. As a child I drew a beard on my face with red ink and this new beard was transposed upon a pillow. The seas are red with beards.

California: the brief story of a whale's beard.

She says my beard tickles her lips. She slips a valentine into my mouth.

My beard of red. Her hair of ashes, not flames. Her valentine: the forced laughter of the bearded lady or the constant quiet of her only son? I will shave quickly, at my leisure, at night, under a tree.

The rumor of an eternal beard. The moon is the face of madness (it has no beard). My false beard is drained of color as I dream.

There is a beard of untapped potential on the face of the dead assassin, the beard of Joseph Stalin is now twice the size of Russia, and I have a beard of false confessions that I tuck into my shirt at night—every beard has its thorn.

Bury your heads in the beard of sorrow, people. I shall sink my teeth into the beard of sorrows past.

"They will bury us next to our beards."

My lord has a beard that goes all the way to his belly. A ridiculous beard and mine's just like it.

Winter Outtakes (2)

A man goes from barren tree to tree, threatening to chop down each. "I am sure that this tree will be as heavy with fruit next spring," he says, "as I am heavy with grief this day."

What I hear are the somnambulists coming down the hall. About eight of them. They're quick. Right now everything smells like buttermilk, but the world is still distant to me, like a cloud to its shadow. I'm the shadow. Of something bigger. I think. Like the memo says: the world is merely a path made visible and we are allotted only so much time to be strangled by it. So my advice is to go out there and raise some hell. Like the somnambulists. The fat one dreams he's cutting a dangerous path through Arkansas back before anyone even bothered calling it Arkansas, when everyone stayed up all night smoking and worrying about the new shit popping up on the maps, when a disease could spread across a city like coffee spilled on a map. This fat one moves quickly because in his dream there's less history to drag around. I find this genuinely moving.

I've never seen anyone sleepwalk before, not even in a movie, but one night a few years previous I was up very late (this was after I finished my second pot of coffee and twelfth sonnet) and watched a film I made years before; it was of a snowstorm in reverse (after forty minutes I was genuinely moved by a sudden glimpse of the green lawn) accompanied by the sound of a woman I, once upon a time, knew intimately: the sound of her breathing.

I love trivia.

Did you know that Rick James and Neil Young played together in a band called The Mynah Birds? Did you know that Thomas Jefferson was once given a 1,235-pound hunk of cheese, giving us the term "the big cheese?" That sleepwalkers are not allowed in the armed services because of the threat they pose when they have access to dangerous equipment and are unaware of what they are doing? I have razors hidden throughout my room, so I'm curious as to what will happen when all the somnambulists get in here.

3

As I flew through the windshield I knew being nice did not always work like magic. Listen to this, Agnes: right now my auto-biography is well-hid. I can't find it. The furniture's been moved. Jose Medina says it was a no-passing zone and that my only hope is to be reached immediately. Prayers are long goodbyes/greetings from a casino/a way to go touching. As I flew through the blank comedy I knew mathematical beauty. I can get away with going through a windshield because windows bring symmetry. Put your hand on a window and you get to know the real world. Put your hand through a window and you study the real world. Put your head

on my shoulder. Suppose that instead of stitching all five senses together along their edges we landed in West Memphis with a month of bad weather and brown carpet on our floors. Agnes, the river is looking for interns and I can feel your tongue in my ear. When we left Europe there were graves to be dug and we were ravenous for an entire night. Like corpses who must rise and walk until they find a bed that fits: on the winter road we contemplated weakness. As I flew through the windshield I saw moths pinned and I saw moths in white plastic buckets, hunting for light. Intimacy arrives with practice—when I landed in the field the sound was half water.

I want to go touching. As I gaze at the soldiers drinking on the rooftop it feels like a different century. Jose Medina is correct in his disdain: the doctors are absolutely modern. They are small children, lost and wandering in their coffins. When the soldiers started shooting dogs in the streets I knew we were on the road again. As I flew through the illustrious night I knew I was a gambler. If the sky is so wonderful why must it hold its summits behind barbed wire? How much music can that air take? How do you like my driving? Agnes, when we spent that summer in your backseat your hands were wise in their violence, your lips wise as whips. Like assassins, the doctors are perfectly modern and have no further questions.

As I flew through the windshield I knew.

Will we gather at the bottom of the lake wrapped in white plastic, hunting for light? The field was wet and familiar. Strange bird, I hear you call me in your sleep. I am in the woods already, like a wolf. Like an assassin, kneeling in the flowers.

Dear Eternity,

As far as kisses go, we screamed when you captured us, trembled when you walked under the cherry tree. We're rarely interesting. We are often necessary. You speak so softly, strange and hunted.

We talked about going to church. "I'm too old to daydream about trains," I said, and I meant, simply, that I'm too old. She read the newspaper quietly and I said, in a serious voice, "There is so much trouble in the world." She unbuttoned her shirt and, through her apparatus, said, "I have dreamed of standing guard with you, near a river, shining our flashlights on those who wash upon the shore." I never liked to discuss these things, our dreams and her speaking through a machine, but now I feel that I must. We talked and (bruises had been sprouting on our legs like light-green dandelions) a word would come through the machine in a manner that surprised us both. We lay on the couch together and slept so we could wake and tell each other our dreams; she said the machine made the dreams sound different, like they were no longer hers. This made her happy because it made difficult things easier to talk about, such as having an affair in a dream, running behind a pickup and jumping into the bed to be with another lover. She said it was strange because she could still see me. "It felt like going down the new I-60," she said, "and seeing the old highway 60 still over there on the right hand side with no one driving on it." I said maybe I was driving the truck and she started into a coughing spell, causing the machine to vibrate, and when the machine went "oh" "Oh" through its speakers, I kept one hand on it as I leaned over to kiss her lips. I forgot the terminology the physician used to describe how the machine works, but at one point, he compared the human voice to a magnet. Later, he compared it to a blizzard; when he did this, he spoke through the machine, for emphasis.

This still makes me laugh.

I felt, tonight, as though I was the night, brought up poorly, puffy and blue in the face, the moon askew on my worn-out pajama top. My enemies came one night when I was young; they wandered around my little crib and tried, with their unseen hands, my mouth and ears, seeking out some crevice by which to enter. My mother at first kept them away with a broom, the broom being a symbol of purification, a magical protection against evil spirits who love dirt. Soon, she used the broom to keep me away as well, though I was unschooled and afraid.

Often, a creature kept me company; some form of dog or wolf with a chestnut coat sprinkled with specks of white velvet. But soon this creature abandoned me as well and I was dragged by my enemies from place to place for examination. I was thrown about and subjected to cruel insults. I faced a gallows courtyard and a lime pit used to reduce the corpses of the condemned.

But if I was tortured like a saint, I grew to become a saint.

What does a saint do? It wails and howls to issue forth, stalks the aisles, glides around pillars, tempts the deepest organs of misery, and, soaring up to the moon, it strives to fling itself defiantly upon the stones below as it passes, muttering, into the memories of men.

This is not all.

We stand on the stairs of the apartment and watch the mountain. We live beneath a lump thrown up in joy. We wiggle a lot when we can't move our hands. We get sleepy. The church is empty, but we stick around. We know where to sit. Plus, who cares? Everyone's taking their time on the winding roads. Life's in the parking lots: everybody leaves something behind and nobody cares about shadows because nobody's a ghost. The skyscrapers go all the way to the horizon. It's like getting to see the shiny spots in our souls. Any notion of The Beginning should be discarded like an onion in a box of tomatoes, but we're making a river to build a bridge across.

And the woman calling "and I let the fish go," hoping it might be so. I saw nobody coming, so I went instead still clinging to your shirt of lost connections. A man of actions dials the telephone during the act, when our minds tend to wander back to the ordinary eye, the cauldron of morning. You take and drop my hand as though it soared suchwise through heaven too. It well may be. I do not think I would like priceless treasures sinking in the sand, in the cedar limbs.

Unawares

1.

"The last three times I went outside," he says, "I didn't want to come back in." He says it as if it's a front yard one can walk around in. Call him Tony, he stands beneath the tree with a tape measure, plans to measure the average distance between the highest plum and every other plum on the tree, as if he and his tree are completed thoughts.

2.

A severed finger may or may not have its own ghost of finger-like size. Tony's thoughts settle to a hum. The tree has bees. The thought of measuring the distance from himself and each of the plums vibrates through Tony. He does not want to romanticize himself and measure from his heart, or (as Agnes suggests) from his crotch, or even his head (Agnes has read that the thinking process is dispersed over the entire nervous system) for he would be choosing which part of his body most fully houses his *I*. He thinks with his eyes. His body is blind. He's obsessed with the tree, because let's face it, poems are not made of words, but paper.

3.

My people are dwindling away all unawares.

This phrase has been written, a star next to it; there are notes in the upper-left corner, in pencil. All this in Tony's handwriting. He does not recall making such notations. He's not even sure why he has starred the above phrase: there are more striking ones, in style and thought, all around it. Yet, *Unawares* will be the title of his project.

4.

The average distance between the highest plum and all the other plums, Tony proposes, will be around his height, unless he counts the plums in the tall grass. Within the alphabet, each letter in *Unawares* is an average of 10.714 letters from the other letters in the word: *u* is seven letters from *n,* etc. Yet all the letters reside comfortably within the word, like plums in a tree, only no falling out, no going bare in winter. Measuring plums is difficult logistically, yet, theoretically, a breeze: each part of the plum is as fully plum as any other. Plus, plums (like letters) are small. Tony uses the pit of each plum as the measuring point, adding a half-inch twice to each measured distance. Letters aren't measured but lined up, like a baby's toes, *a* to *z.* One must only count how many letters come between. This would make measuring the distance between plums unreliable: two plums on the same branch (plum 1 and plum 2, from the left) might be three inches apart, and since there are no plums in between, they would be one plum apart. Plum 3 is one branch up from the first two, a foot away, yet is also only one plum away from plum 2 despite being four times farther away than plum 1 is from plum 2, in inches. Tony's hunch: similar incongruities exist in the alphabet; that *m* and *n* are like plums 1 and 2: not only in proximity sequentially, but also spatially: *n* looks like an echo of *m.* They make similar sounds, causing Tony to believe they are related. In *solemn,* they join seamlessly. Tony finds his parallel to plums 2 and 3 in *x* and *y.* He sang the alphabet song and noticed the pause (space) between *wx* and *y and z.* Something missing. In *xylophone, x* loses its identity and sounds like *z,* making Tony think that *x* and *y* are perhaps on different branches.

5.

A round planet complicates things; there are two ways to measure the distance between two objects: plums 1 and 2, from left to right, are three inches away; yet, from right to left (measuring from plum 1) (Tony would have to go around the globe to measure) they are over 128 million feet (the earth's circumference minus four inches plus half an inch twice) away. If two objects are nearby in one direction, then a world separates them in the other: the ghost-distance. Tony thinks the alphabet is a circle: what comes after *z?*

6.

"Perhaps," Tony thinks, "this would explain the distance between *x* and *y*." He walks into his bedroom. Agnes is asleep; before him is another Tony. This one looks like a ghost and patiently writes in Tony's notebook. Tony reads the questions:

Does an entire alphabet separate m *and* n?

Is there an alphabetical equivalent of fallen plums?

Does this mean nothing is ever really touching?

Tony steps back. He guesses that he is about four steps from Agnes, five or six from his ghost. He leaves the room, begins counting his steps thirteen fourteen fifteen sixteen seventeen across the front lawn eighteen nineteen twenty twenty-one twenty-two twenty-three twenty-four twenty-five twenty-six twenty-seven down the driveway twenty-eight twenty-nine thirty thirty-one thirty-two across the road thirty-three over the ditch thirty-four thirty-five over the neighbor's fence thirty-six thirty-seven thirty-eight thirty-nine forty forty-one forty-two through the neighbor's garden forty-three forty-four forty-five forty-six forty-seven forty-eight into the woods

We're always shoulder to shoulder: you over there, me in here, singing, holding an apple and a knife and you're staring at your wrists: I'm mock-serious (with my knife, knife, knife) and full of ordinary secrets, and you're over there, next to me, with your thousand and one shadows as I, up here (under you) trace the shadows with this knife that you kept, for luck, in your room.

I found it.

The Man in the Gorilla Suit

See if he's sitting with his binoculars in his car, watching us act creepy. Then see if he compares our lips to those of a marble statue. That familiar sidewalk feel. Light collects around our feet, or night hides beneath our feet, or rather, we sink

like dolls into happy shadows, in synch with the tree-line curving towards the sea. We walk at night, comfy with those things night-like, but still looking at them in daylight, as if cars didn't come with headlights. Moths, attracted to the sidewalk, flutter around our feet. The hour

is deadly. Girls walking home from movies. But our darker purposes are not our real ones: our sinks are full of yellow plates, good men walk the sidewalk. There is more light than ever. We see its reflection all the time. Our subject, still in his car, reflects on this, and he's pleased that *light* and *night*

still rhyme. "Is the sun a poor gesture of night?" he asks. "Am I a jester in the court of no-light?" Like bees, our paths are classic ones, gathering. But without a car one is not a mechanic. We discover this as we sink into the shadows, which, we soon see, are painfully boring. But the sidewalk

is where the real hurting takes place. We walk to keep from crying, dancing all night, one mouth on top of the other. I'll see if I can follow you. I mean, we describe our cars without telling anyone where we're going. The sun sinking is an old story, sure, but night will soon be touching cars,

mouths, black forests, etc. What's farthest away from, say, a car, is, on a round surface, what's also touching it. Sidewalks could not be any further from the streets, our sinks are far from their sunny plates. So? So if we love the night we should not embrace it. Think of the distance behind us. Our

gaze should probably return to the man in the car, or maybe the sea surrounding his car. The sea inside it. The sea itself.

Swans of Local Waters

Their color is not a product of the water's depth; their quiet is not the lake's. These are accidents floating in simple water, taking in nature calmly, in little sips; actions which, like literal swans and lakes, are sometimes scattered. What the swans look like: white, with feathers. It's getting cold. Someone has made a fire. A flame's identity depends upon what it burns—identity is like a swan for it comes and goes as it pleases.

I don't know how to talk about my biological father, so I am going to describe the lake: it's blue, with swans. I can film it. There's still a fire by the lake. The swans are safe in the water. It's getting cold. Almost dark. I have a list of things that get more definite at night.

1) The shape of fire.
2)

4

Some folks are unable to talk on the phone in a noisy office or airport while others can make a call from anywhere. Some folks break the phone because they are afraid it will ring. My father feared the ferry-boat that took us to our summer vacation home; when the horn blew he would throw himself on an imaginary sword. During my lifetime, I've made at least 200, 000 observations. For example, clouds often just disappear.

When women think about abstract concepts like love or death, they use visual images, such as a sliding glass door. For example, a romance must be approached gently for barging forward too quickly may shatter the door. Some women enjoy watching automatic sliding doors for they receive the same feelings of pleasure that occur when they engage in kissing or other, typically romantic, behaviors. My father told me how he gently encouraged my mother to tolerate more and more kissing; one evening she was held in a light kiss until her weeping lessened, then she was released.

He sent me a video describing the squeeze machine he's developing to satisfy his craving for the feeling of being held. "You know," he says, "not everything has to be touched."

Some trains go over three hundred miles per hour without ever touch-ing the tracks. Some people insist on wearing pants for they dislike the feeling of their legs touching. Those who cannot tolerate talking can be desensitized by a gentle rubbing of the mouth.

Twelve Self Portraits

1.

The snow is dark and nothing is sad and I was, once upon a time, a child. I knew what the weather meant, was hardened the way only a child, after all, is.

The first ten years are full of rain. I watched the shadows flee away.

The snow is something else, tonight, as I stand, grown, naked (I'm in the living room, the lights are off): invisible and filling up.

2.

That's me, tongue placed firmly in the subconscious. A slow undercurrent, a breath (twisting). Silent I suppose, and sad.

It is my time (in this, my second self portrait, I am unapologetically ill and in my early eighties) and I call to my side my large circle of friendly landscapes and intimate portraits and willingly take my leave of them. Also, the fringe elements of me: the street performer and the recluse, the terminally hip and the lost child (yes I am still looking into the dreams of that child, manipulating them, trying to recover some lost humanity in the process).

3.

Like that of a swimmer amongst the drowning, this face expresses longing and mischief. I am trying to hint at solitude. We would together, her and I, grab hold a piece of his garment, if only to meditate upon each change of expression as he began to drown. We would praise his performance. In his face were railroads and banks, mills and pity for the riches found there. What is it this face says now? That we are all blue flame and frost, all milk and mystery? That we each should breathe also the upper air? (I gaze upon actual faces in meditative hours and am reminded that we are not transparent despite the brute light that shines through.)

4.

Pain is a higher awareness of self.

Here is my fourth portrait, touched by the hand of mayhem.

She's in it. She stands before me and strips away time and lamentation. Her right hand points at the journey of the stars, at each unwilling horse.

5.

In this one I sketch for her my hounded heart. Exhausted and dizzy, we are lifted until our voices are no more rank to us than death is.

Staying awake is a punishment (every day I was awake this year). Once upon a time, she told me a ghost story: how she hit darkness on the highway one night, how I was the thumbprint of that tiny crash.

6.

This is my portrait and I am one of its citizens. I wake, take brief repose, confess a little tooth and claw, compose and perform a priestly shriek. And she trusts me. My news is tolerable.

All I swallow becomes mine, becomes good. Whatever interests my voice interests me: a belly, a room of strangers, a puff of smoke. They are asking me questions.

I hear them.

I'm coming back to this room (to get things straight). A room is instructed by its kings so I've begun drawing crowns and getting angry easily, which comes from caring too much. Often, the size of the heart determines the size of the emotion. The small pleasures of birds, for instance.

7.

There is a prayer folded in my mouth; like the night, it wanders as it searches for its bride. There are no shortcuts around this mountain (a prayer is a mountain, looking for its bride). But there is a mountain.

8.

A bridge will be written —Hart Crane

A face will be written. Another year will be written, with each of its hostile devils. A redemption will be performed as it is composed. The heights will be written, if only for the slave of tears to gaze at them in dissatisfaction.

The slave of tears has already been written.

He speaks for the room, the river, the air. He speaks to the heights because he wants to. A fine trembling will be written. The heights will be written. An answer will be written, and an embrace.

9.

Perhaps every little thing must be recovered if anything is to be saved. Here are my eyes. They do not wish to be frozen by the wintry light of understanding. Happily, I (like a flame) understand nothing. At a conspiring hour, I am standing under the birches, in winter, learning to hunt.

10.

A portrait is also a path made visible. The world is an ally of the visible.

I am sitting in the meadow grass scratching doubt and belief. I think a lot of people have grown up with a peek at the future, with songs never recorded. My goal is simple: to play jacks in front of the levee. (I desire to be not only graceful, but visible. Useful. I do not desire the wisdom of the worm, nor of the hook.) To become timeless.

So how *do* we die, really? And what *is* the exact location of the cross-roads? I'm not predisposed towards elevating things beyond what we see and touch, but by the time I noticed I was crossing this field, I knew the living must communicate with life.

11.

The journey into our bodies is another journey, like the night: as long as a riddle. Gristle, and grace. When she was a child, no one would cut her hair for her. It went down to her waist.

My childhood was a river as well, one to drag my faith across; my hair floated in the water behind me. My eyes were painted shut and the clouds were boats.

And is she still barefoot, without a thing in her hands? Is she wading in clouds? ("Like God, we dream only of rivers.")

I am trying to draw the lumps in our throats. The ones we had when we were born, when we finally die. The ones that mean: *I will not remember this.*

12.

The snow is thick and I have just found a wolf; it's an actual wolf. I name it Broken Mirror. I can see its ribs. I take it inside and teach it how to count. The wolf's heart is a thing of rhythms, a thing of sand. I carry it from room to room; the wolf seems to be swallowing its tongue. "My voice carries," I say. "It will carry you."

I bury the night in the morning. In the morning the flowers grow. Then I cut the flowers and bury them too. Then I get something to eat. I'm the Ted Williams of darkness: a natural at it, I devote hours. I believe in maintaining a generous balance between all things. This includes balance and imbalance. This includes night and night. It's that time, the 25th hour. The hour of blood-going-dry in the cattle. The hour of the singular valley. That's why I'm standing on the roof, swinging at the pitch, swinging for the fences.

"But we're gonna be huge," the night tells me, softly, like a wounded machine.

"But you're supposed to lead me out of private labyrinths and into eternal ones," I say, sleepily, like a hungry dog.

"Some nights build churches and some nights build wars," the night answers, muttering to itself.

Tonight is both of those nights. Tonight is neither of those nights because it's an elegant and wintry morning, Sunshine. For years I've slept as my body was passed from night to night to night, from Tinker to Evers to Chance.

I don't remember her answer to my secret question. I'm sure she was pretty and happy. I have a hard time remembering things from the months before my parents drove me across the state and left me there. I don't truly recall all the kids running, or the one child who ripped his clothes, tore at them madly.

In this daze and darkness, I don't remember falling asleep. But I remember waking up.

The perhaps most important reason why people forget their dreams is that they don't care.

I remember crying a lot in class. I don't remember my user name. I knew her from I don't remember which class but I do remember that it was on the pretext of talking about this class that we stepped away from the crowd.

I remember bringing in a penny for every inch of my life. I remember bringing home dead animals to study and my mother being very encouraging. I do not remember bringing the lit end of a cigarette to my face and burning myself, although I do remember driving my car into her darkened bedroom, which is when screaming became more than a hobby for her.

I barely remember my own name most of the time, let alone what I have done to other people, so all these scars do help me organize my thoughts a little.

Apparently, it is Monday. Somebody called me first thing this morning and told me I could sleep again.

It's like waking up and kissing a mirror good morning. The challenge is finding a reason. One approach is holding onto the ball, staying in bounds, waiting for the clock to run out. There are lots of reasons strutting around, flapping their wings, but they are often stupid reasons. Entire towns sell their souls for any number of reasons; people die for one, maybe two reasons. I have a pet chicken. Echo. He is my favorite chicken. Had him since I was a child (first chicken best chicken). The night is a black moth. A spoon grazing my lips. The night is a black mouth. I have killed my favorite chicken. The night is a black month or a red month. It's late. A man passes a door three or four times before he realizes it's the way out.

Crossing a Bridge Sweetens the Body

My shadow is down there in the water, making soft little noises. I was born holding a demon's hand. This is why I always enter a room dancing. My song has alternated between the song of a dog tied to a post and the song of linear subordination. I'm working on a new song. It goes: "I won't hurt you, I won't hurt you, I won't hurt you."

5

In a lot of ways this is a children's story. The basic plot is simple; most of it is told from a well. My own children dwell in a city, have no little spoon-tree, no two or three moon-trees overshadowing rosebushes, just the parlor windows enveloped in the light snow, which makes a kind of wintry here-and-there.

If one evening or street passes by, another shall come.

There is always the transformation of environmental events into either eternal or internal regularities, but a wind still comes in the early evening hours and the stars and moons get stacked like the colors of a tin cup.

The length of time human skin can tolerate various temperatures depends upon pigmentation. Theoretically, gold or silver skin would outlast the sun by a few seconds. And we all love the sun. I hope it will stay and be repaired and renewed over the years, that no council or planning scheme will remove it. No wonder my children sit lingering over a cup of coffee until sunset. Just good manners to let us older ones know who's still a series of loud hums, who's a crackle or two, who's coating the streets with that white imitation snow that comes in spray bottles.

A method to conversation: invoking at times what other people say, at times what one thinks on one's own, and the two mixed together like a couple of kids beneath a sheet, a shared skin. Talking becomes a conscious stammering not in one's language, but in how one thinks; a conversation represents not so much a break with solitude, but a newer form of solitude, a revision of the logic of solitude.

I said: "You are a wave."

She said: "I touch you once and then carry you away."

One is not condemned to a perpetual present, nor to the immediacy of seemingly random, unconnected signifiers. In summary, one is here because one has remembered to be here. In conversation, one discusses what rises. War? There's no doubt the public likes to see victims, if only to patronize them with applause. Sleep? It is not difficult to sleep. The sea? A man in the ocean is awash in blue thoughts.

My blind dog smiles often, has small shoulders. He grinds his teeth when I lecture him. Agnes regarded him as most would a storm. He left little green snakes on her side of the bed. He would show her his teeth and wiggle his ears at her.

He answers to my name, and his. We both have noble origins. We share a certain stillness.

Last night, my blind dog went to the bridge.

He likes it by the lake, would answer to whatever name I needed to call him by: Champ, Blue, Lucky, Danger, Shadow, Swede. His howl brings a terrible splash to my belly. He has a nightingale in his throat.

"If you cannot see my mirrors," the man in the truck says, "then I cannot see you."

Identity is an accident arising from the weaknesses of others: I own a blind dog, Agnes could not stay, my neighbors do not see me boarding this train.

The phone, last night, rang. Not much of a sound on the other line (a cloud brushing against another cloud on a cold, cold night). An empty house begs for a small, slow story. When I discovered my dog was blind, I mourned for weeks, walked through parking lots, ran my nails through my beard, asked others my name.

My dog cannot see me with his eyes so he sees me with his heart. Mine own eyes are dim. I could not faint last night, on the porch. It hardly matters. My blind dog is searching for me even as we speak. I will be found, even though he will not see my reaction, although I will not hear the ticks.

A father may be the author of a man's form, but not his essence: that is the jurisdiction of the unknown. If a father attempts to be the author of both form and essence, then the father seeks not to be a father, but the unknown, and thus a god and must be devoured. When Bob Dylan was a boy and stole his father's matches he knew this. Also, when he was then chained to a door.

I know it too, but often forget, especially in times like right now, when I'm breaking into some dude's house and stealing his stereo. In these moments, my thoughts are usually of obligation; as a thief, it's my obligation, after breaking into a house, to take something of value. It is also my obligation to leave (the wound's obligation to ache but also to heal).

Obligation is a chair in the woods: an idealized form placed in the natural world, out-of-place and perhaps even a perversion of its "roots," but still something to be sought, reupholstered, and then used, if only as an agent of rest.

Or, obligation is an extra hand. Something to be severed.

When I was ten I broke into my father's office to steal some money and there he was, digitally stimulating my mother and talking on the phone. Agnes said I have spent my life's capital perpetually sneaking into my father's office, then telling myself I was a trespasser of the unknown.

"The ancient male ritual of penetrating the public sphere only to stumble upon a penetration of the private one," she said.

Like Dylan's sons: their father wrote a song about a river once, so now they run all over the house and look for it.

The world is liquid, every sound a splash, each highway a different shade of blue. I am a scientist. She gets in the mood. She gets into the tempo and ten years pass and I find out that I'm actually a river: I can only taste her if she's in my mouth.

I am married to what we call distance, a hundred miles of night from one end of the house to the other. Nights lined up, one after the other, like shirts for sale. She likes it on the floor. I prefer the closet.

Like the man said: the best questions aren't. I am holding her breath. She is pretending to float.

To Lean on a Broken Reed

1.

The dude creeps beneath the low branches and flowers. The girl with the hair walks up to him, but she does not dance or sing; instead she wheels towards and addresses the night:

"There is something frantic, both in his optimism, and in your desire to bear witness to something optimistic. At best, his mood is musical. I, however, am as calm as a glass of milk, even now beneath this sky."

2.

Two blue trains pass in the fog. The dude boards one and sleeps for seven days and nights; some nights last a thousand years. The dude awakes in Texarkana and walks to the VFW hall, where the lights are dim and dancers sway to "Moonlight Serenade." It's the coldest summer on record.

"My life," he says, "contains not only many famous dreams, but also has its origins in a dream."

It's late and the sky is imprinted with the first few kisses of light. He walks on; the inappropriateness of the hour is a temptation for him to sing; it's like the excitement of a quarrel. The girl is alone. She was raised here. She wraps her overcoat tightly and, as the dude ascends the sloping road, she listens. She has a warm and windowless heart, a secret to tell, but she lets him pass, unwilling to interfere with any form of pilgrimage.

"To learn to think," she whispers to herself, "one should also consult those who hate thoughts."

3.

At the top of the mountain, the dusk spills music and birds.

"At the close of things," the dude tells the girl, "the unknown does not, as we would prefer, become lucid, but rather, merely less unimaginable—but in times of ending one gets distracted by names, flowers, dead batteries."

The girl has streaks in her hair. And red boots. The dude:

"At the close of things, a man finds himself solitary and ladylike as he rings the bells of jubilee."

The mountain at dusk looks like a cloud at night.

"At the close of things," the girl responds, "I through my garden shall go, to Lake Magic and Lake Pleasure, in my hood of clouds."

Let me return to my original theory: we are sleeping in the fires our enemies have started. The flames are like honey; a bit sticky, a bit strange in the mouth.

Tell them (remember, they are your enemies as much as mine): tell them the silence of the dead is not a sign of forgetfulness on the dead's part, nor weariness, nor neglect. The dead are singing, though we have no dead. When my enemies take my head and throw it in the fire I will sing ("I Am Damo Suzuki," "I Am the Cosmos"), even as my family is slaughtered.

But this is incorrect.

I have always lived alone—have I not? Deserted, rolling in and out of clouds of boredom?

When I was barely ten years old I quit school. I had to learn the names of people from whom I derived no profit, yet if I slipped up in naming, I was whipped, burned or banished, for those were the methods approved by my enemies. Though the teachers were on my side, they had no other end in view. It was as if they were river merchants in waters of divine providence, even they admitted such.

When I was accused of avoiding study, it was true. It was not for want of aptitude, but sheer love of avoidance.

6

I listened to the jackals breathing in the high grass and wondered how anyone could imagine a quiet shade for the sleepers. The river is rising. If death speaks, it does not speak to us. (If a jackal is seen, it is night.) I, too, shall wear my own howling. But tonight I am dressed like a man. I run gently and pleasantly, confidence stealing into me: the longer I gaze at the beautiful and strange, the more the river rises. I am a mysterious walker. I was once a small place filled with hats. (Time is conquered through time, where the river is widest.)

Where the river is widest one can see the mud flats and broad stretches of green marsh grass. This is a sad kind of thing, like watching a child, a woman, a clown, a moralist from a century ago be crushed by a thousand hidden eyes. The river rises and runs down the same slope where I first heard orchestral excerpts of the wilderness: jackals trembling, but only from the cold. I run gently and pleasantly towards the actual: solitude is here, metaphors of death and flow, a cloud factory (built in '75), small slides, torn cats. The right side belongs to the dogs and the left to the jackals. My friends are wheels turning away from themselves.

Turning away from themselves, the summers are torched by hand. Fall breaks through the branches, moves on, leaves me with a handful of pocketknives and a ringing phone on the counter. It's always night upstairs. Either this rising goes, or I do. I have to be careful where I lie down, on which side of the river I gather. My friends are wearing their crushes and their crushes are going bad. We share our codeine, jackals, bourbon. Good night, my darklings, I am about to—or I am going to—become a great leap in the dark. Either expression is correct. Get my swan costume ready, I'll be in Texas when the sun is out.